CONTENTS

ABOUT HATCHES

I often hear new fly fishers ask, *"What in (the heck, tarnation, the name of Rudyard Kipling, etc.) is a hatch?"* Answer: a hatch is a migration of insects abandoning their underwater lives to fly and mate up in the air. A proper hatch consists of one specific kind of insect—not just mayflies, for example, but *March Brown* mayflies. Somehow, these March Browns all agree to hatch at about the same time—a few minutes to a few hours each day over weeks or months. Most hatching insects make this same agreement. The result is a concentration of easy prey that stirs trout to serious feeding.

It may stir them to *single-minded* feeding as well. Happens all the time; it's just the way trout are. Consequently, our hypothetical trout will now refuse any fly that doesn't look and behave like a March Brown.

That's where this booklet comes in—it helps you identify a hatching insect (the March Brown included), select an appropriate fly to match it, and fish that fly effectively. And it does a lot more besides.

Not all hatches are here—there are *scads* of hatching insect species. But the ones you'll encounter again and again, the critical hatches, *are* here.

So that's the nature and the importance of insect hatches, and why this booklet—designed to fit in a pocket and be carelessly thumbed with wet hands—can draw more trout to your flies.

INTRODUCTION TO MAYFLIES

Near the end of a life, until now, spent entirely under water, a mayfly transforms for flight as it emerges into the air; transforms once more; mates; flies out (if it is a female) to release its fertilized eggs back into the water (to which it usually falls exhausted); and after just a few days or even hours of flitting on wings, dies. The underwater stage is the *nymph,* the first winged stage is the *dun,* and the final and fully mature stage is the *spinner.* Most mayfly species swim right up to hatch out in the perilous open (for which trout are forever grateful).

The chief identifying features of the mayfly are its upright softly triangular wings and long, fine tails.

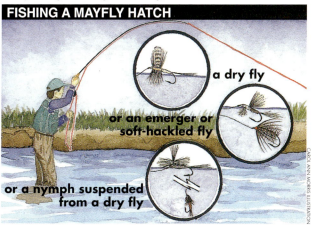

FISHING A MAYFLY HATCH

a dry fly

or an emerger or
soft-hackled fly

or a nymph suspended
from a dry fly

CAROL ANN MORRIS ILLUSTRATION

5

Mayfly

BAETIS
(*Baetis tricaudatus* and others)

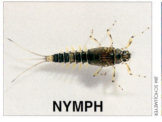

JIM SCHOLLMEYER

NYMPH

JIM SCHOLLMEYER

DUN

Usually referred to by its genus name, *Baetis,* sometimes as the Blue-Winged Olive, this is truly the any-day mayfly of streams. While most mayflies hatch only once or twice for a few weeks each year, the tiny *Baetis* hatches the year round (though not very dependably). All western streams contain it. The experienced fly fisher, whenever he or she fishes in streams, half expects a hatch of Blue-Winged Olives. And should.

center tail
short or absent

light-olive to
dark-brown

light-gray or
blueish-olive

two tails

pale- to dark-olive

CAROL ANN MORRIS ILLUSTRATIONS

Important Stages: dun, emerger
Occasionally Important: nymph, spinner
Seasonal Hatch Time: year round. Peaks vary
Daily Hatch Time: 11:00 a.m. to 4:00 p.m.
Hatch Conditions: overcast, even stormy best. But sunny can be good
Size: body 1/8 to 5/16 inch (3-7 mm). Hooks 22-16

actual size (all stages)

INCHES

MAXIMUM

MINIMUM

0   1/4   1/2   3/4   1

Habitat: slow to lively currents. Rocks, debris, water plants
Fishing Strategies: a dry fly dead drift to rising trout is standard and effective. Also effective is a dead-drift emerger or nymph (the nymph suspended just a few inches down)
Note: smaller (to size-24 hooks) *Acentrella* looks like *Baetis* and hatches afternoons, June through September. Fish it just as you would *Baetis*

Baetis **Typical Imitative Flies**

Troth Pheasant Tail   *Baetis* **Soft Hackle**   **Parachute Adams**

FLIES TIED AND PHOTOGRAPHED BY SKIP MORRIS

Mayfly

WESTERN MARCH BROWN
(*Rhithrogena*)

NYMPH

DUN

To many Western fly fishers, the March Brown's arrival heralds the first serious trout fishing of the year. Winter still may linger, but substantial mayflies drifting among the noses of hungry trout on rivers yet unswollen by melting snow is a vision to warm the fisherman on chilly days. Near the end of the season a second hatch, lesser but often still strong, may come to echo late winter's good crisp fishing.

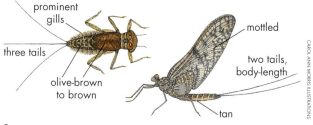

prominent gills

three tails

olive-brown to brown

mottled

two tails, body-length

tan

CAROL ANN MORRIS ILLUSTRATIONS

Important Stages: dun, emerger

Occasionally Important: nymph

Seasonal Hatch Time: March through June, September

Daily Hatch Time: 11:00 a.m. to 4:00 p.m.

Hatch Conditions: mild and overcast best. Heavy, brief hatch on sunny days

Habitat: among rocks in lively currents

Size: body 5/16 to 1/2 inch (8-12 mm). Hooks 16-10

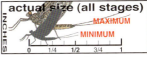

actual size (all stages)
INCHES
MAXIMUM
MINIMUM
0   1/4   1/2   3/4   1

Fishing Strategies: the hatch usually occurs in slower water next to quick. A dry fly dead drift to rising trout is standard. Other options: an emerger, or a nymph suspended a few inches down, both dead drift.

Also good: a soft-hackle fly barely coaxed across the current

Western March Brown Typical Imitative Flies

Gold Ribbed Hare's Ear   March Brown Spider   March Brown Sparkle Dun

Mayfly

WESTERN GREEN DRAKE
(*Ephemerella grandis*)

NYMPH

JIM SCHOLLMEYER

DUN

CAROL ANN MORRIS

The Green Drake hatch is an event. This mayfly is big enough to draw large trout to the surface and, consequently, maintain a devoted following of anglers—devoted enough to come despite the risk of missing this brief and undependable hatch. Part of the attractiveness of the Green Drake to trout (and, therefore, to anglers) is its dallying atop the water—a long and perilous ride giving trout the advantage.

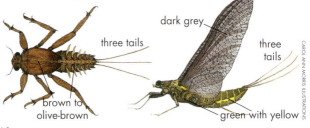

three tails

brown to olive-brown

dark grey

three tails

green with yellow

CAROL ANN MORRIS ILLUSTRATIONS

Important Stages: dun, emerger. (Few anglers imitate the nymph; the spinner comes after dark)
Seasonal Hatch Time: late May through July
Daily Hatch Time: 11:00 a.m. to 4:00 p.m.
Hatch Conditions: longest hatches with overcast, shorter with sunshine

Size: body 1/2 to 3/4 inch (12-19 mm). Hooks 12-8

actual size (all stages)

INCHES

MAXIMUM

MINIMUM

0   1/4   1/2   3/4   1

Habitat: rocks and debris in quick currents
Fishing Strategies: a dry fly or emerger fished dead drift to rising trout

Western Green Drake Typical Imitative Flies

Green Drake Emerger

Green Drake

FLIES TIED AND PHOTOGRAPHED BY SKIP MORRIS

Mayfly

PALE MORNING DUN
(*Ephemerella inermis* and *infrequens*)

JIM SCHOLLMEYER

NYMPH

JIM SCHOLLMEYER

DUN

Touched with the color of sunshine, the little Pale Morning Dun (also known as the PMD) is the staple of summer mayflies, hatching from the last weeks of spring to as late as early fall. Its hatching is as consistent and dependable as the hatching of mayflies gets.

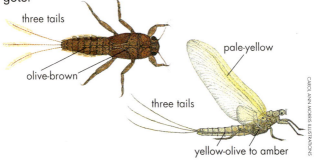

three tails

olive-brown

pale-yellow

three tails

yellow-olive to amber

CAROL ANN MORRIS ILLUSTRATIONS

12

Important Stages: dun, emerger
Occasionally Important: nymph, spinner
Seasonal Hatch Time: late May through September
Daily Hatch Times: 11:00 a.m. to 1:00 p.m. at first, morning and afternoon later
Hatch Conditions: any weather, but longer hatches on cool, over-cast days
Habitat: among rocks and debris in light currents

Size: body 1/4 to 3/8 inch (6 - 9 mm). Hooks 18-14

actual size (all stages)
INCHES
MAXIMUM
MINIMUM
0   1/4   1/2   3/4   1

Fishing Strategies: a dry fly or emerger fished dead-drift to rising trout is standard and effective. A nymph suspended just below a dry fly can be good. Spinners are sometimes important, coming usually in mornings or evenings

Typical Imitative Flies

Skip Nymph
Dark

CDC
Transitional Dun

Light Cahill
Parachute

Mayfly

TRICO
(*Tricorythodes minutus*)

DUN

SPINNER

JIM SCHOLLMEYER

Are Tricos tiny? *Oh* yes. Insignificant? Not necessarily. Wait till you see *Tricorythodes* duns and spinners (the spinners can return while duns are still hatching) so thick on calm currents they lie in tangles. Then you'll understand how so small an insect can be important. Sometimes it's frustrating, trying to get your fly found among hordes of real insects. But always intriguing.

three tails (very long for males)

whitish

female, olive
male, dark-brown

dark-brown

clear wings

dark brown

three tails (very long for males)

female, olive
male, dark-brown

CAROL ANN MORRIS ILLUSTRATIONS

Important Stages: dun, spinner
Seasonal Hatch Time: mid-June through October
Daily Hatch Time: dawn to 12:00 p.m. (Spinners often arrive while duns are still hatching)
Hatch Conditions: none in particular
Size: body 1/8 to 1/4 inch (3-6 mm). Hooks 24-18

Habitat: water plants, silt, and slow currents
Fishing Strategies: early in the hatch a floating emerger or dun imitation is best. If the spinners arrive during the hatch, imitations of emergers, duns, and spinners may all produce. Few anglers fish nymphs during Trico hatches

actual size (all stages)

INCHES

MAXIMUM
MINIMUM

0   1/4   1/2   3/4   1

Trico Typical Imitative Flies

Adams Midge

Trico Poly Wing Spinner

FLIES TIED AND PHOTOGRAPHED BY SKIP MORRIS

INTRODUCTION TO STONEFLIES

The real fishing action in a stonefly hatch is usually inconspicuous. At hatching time, the nymphs creep quietly shoreward, crawl up out of the water, and shed their shucks. This migration exposes the nymphs, and when things really get going, trout move in close to hunt for them.

So stoneflies hatch safe from trout. But trout know that stoneflies are clumsy, that their scrambling and mating can send them tumbling to the water from streamside foliage, and so the trout move in again. Female stoneflies on egg-laying flights are often presented to trout by flying miscalculations or wind.

The adult stonefly is thick-bodied with stout legs, tails, and antennae, and holds its wings flat over its body when at rest.

STONEFLIES

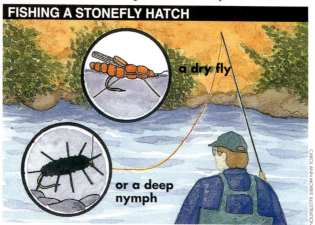

FISHING A STONEFLY HATCH

a dry fly

or a deep nymph

CAROL ANN MORRIS ILLUSTRATION

16

Stonefly

SALMONFLY
(*Pteronarcys*)

NYMPH

JIM SCHOLLMEYER

ADULT

CAROL ANN MORRIS

The Salmonfly's proportions almost rival its reputation—though no real insect could equal the legend. The largest common trout-stream insect of the West (the Golden Stonefly is a close second), the Salmonfly can come off in dazzling numbers. Rivers renowned for their Salmonfly hatches draw crowds of starry-eyed fly fishers from around the world.

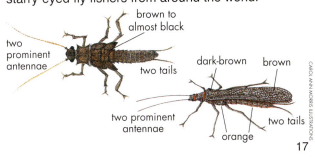

two prominent antennae

brown to almost black

two tails

two prominent antennae

dark-brown

brown

orange

two tails

CAROL ANN MORRIS ILLUSTRATIONS

17

Salmonfly Continued . . .

Important Stages:
nymph, adult

Seasonal Hatch Time:
late May to mid-July

Daily Hatch Time: dusk
through dawn; the actual
hatching is of little importance

Hatch Conditions: any
weather except a cold snap

Size: body 1 to 2 inches (25-
50 mm). Hooks 2-8, long shank

Habitat: around and under
stones in swift water

Fishing Strategies:
because the nymph is enormous
and ever-present in its long cycle
of growth, an imitation always
holds promise. But a nymph is
especially promising mornings
and evenings just before and
during the hatch. Once plenty of
adults are around, cast a dry fly
back into shade
from mid-day till
dark, or toss it out
anywhere on over-
cast days

actual size (all stages)

INCHES

MAXIMUM

MINIMUM

0   1/4   1/2   3/4   1   1/4   1/2   3/4   2

Salmonfly Typical Imitative Flies

Rubber Legs

**Morrisfoam
Salmonfly**

FLIES TIED AND PHOTOGRAPHED BY SKIP MORRIS

18

Stonefly

GOLDEN STONE
(*Calineuria californica* and *Hesperoperla pacifica*)

NYMPH

ADULT

Unjustly overshadowed by the famous Salmonfly, the Golden Stone is nearly as big, just as plentiful, and easier to find. The hatching of these two may overlap (the Salmonfly comes first) speckling stream banks and sky with huge bright and dark insects. The female Golden's habit of dropping to water to release her eggs, unlike the salmonfly's aerial dump, makes the Golden Stone particularly available to trout.

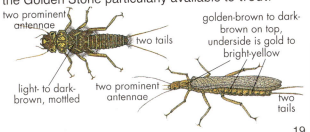

two prominent antennae

two tails

light- to dark-brown, mottled

golden-brown to dark-brown on top, underside is gold to bright-yellow

two prominent antennae

two tails

CAROL ANN MORRIS ILLUSTRATIONS

19

Golden Stone Continued . . .

Important Stages:
nymph, adult
Seasonal Hatch Time:
early June through July
Daily Hatch Time: night,
but the hatch itself is
unimportant
Hatch Conditions: all
weather except a cold spell
Size: body 1 to 1 1/2 inches
(25-38 mm). Hooks 8-4,
long shank

Habitat: around and under
stones in swift water
Fishing Strategies: the
nymph is ever present in
streams that contain it,
due to its two- to three-year
life cycle, and so big
that an imitation is promising any time, but best just
before and during the hatch,
mornings and evenings.
When the adults are plentiful, mid-day to dark can be
great on dry flies, especially
back in shade or on over-
cast days

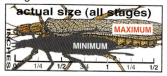

actual size (all stages)

MAXIMUM

MINIMUM

INCHES 0   1/4   1/2   3/4   1   1/4   1/2

Golden Stone Typical Imitative Flies

Matt's Fur

**Improved
Golden Stone**

FLIES TIED AND PHOTOGRAPHED BY SKIP MORRIS

INTRODUCTION TO CADDISFLIES

Mysteriously, most texts on flies and hatches written before the 1970s were really about mayflies, giving caddisflies very little attention. But trout have always been big fans of caddis; authors and anglers were bound to figure that out, and finally did.

Like the midge, and many other aquatic insects, the caddis lives underwater as a *larva* most of its life, then creeps out or swims up (depending on species) as a *pupa,* hatching finally as a winged *adult.* Adult female caddisflies later skim the water (or crawl *under*water) and release their eggs.

The adult caddis has no tails and at rest holds its wings folded over its back in signature tent-fashion.

FISHING A CADDISFLY HATCH

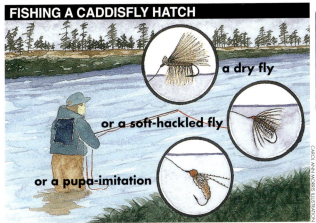

a dry fly

or a soft-hackled fly

or a pupa-imitation

CADDISFLIES

Caddisfly

GRAY SEDGE
(*Rhyacophila*)

LARVA

CAROL ANN MORRIS

PUPA

JIM SCHOLLMEYER

ADULT

JIM SCHOLLMEYER

CADDISFLIES

All three stages of *Rhyacophila*—larva, pupa, and adult—are commonly important to the fly fisher. The larva may abound in swift water where it's often swept to the waiting mouths of trout. The pupa is usually the best stage to imitate during a hatch. The egg-laying adult can draw trout up to slash at dry flies. The Green Rockworm is another common name for the larva, and for *Rhyacophila* in general.

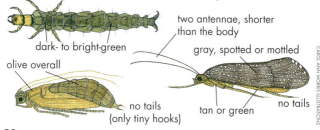

dark- to bright-green

two antennae, shorter than the body

gray, spotted or mottled

olive overall

no tails (only tiny hooks)

tan or green

no tails

CAROL ANN MORRIS ILLUSTRATIONS

22

Important Stages: larva, pupa, adult

Seasonal Hatch Time: late March through early October

Daily Hatch Time: late afternoon to dusk. Egg-laying, afternoon

Hatch Conditions: all weather

Size: body 3/8 to 5/8 inch (10-16 mm). Hooks 14-8

actual size (all stages)
INCHES
MAXIMUM
MINIMUM
0   1/4   1/2   3/4   1

Habitat: among rocks in quick currents

Fishing Strategies: trout in swift water may watch for the larvae, so an imitation always holds promise there. During the hatch a dry fly can be good, but the quick flight of the new adults usually makes pupa- or emerger-flies best. Afternoon egg-laying flights of the females draw trout up to still or skittered dry flies; and to wet flies, when those same caddis swim down to finish their task

FLIES TIED AND PHOTOGRAPHED BY SKIP MORRIS

Gray Sedge Typical Imitative Flies

Green Rockworm

March Brown Spider

Elk Hair Caddis

Caddisfly

SPOTTED SEDGE
(*Hydropsyche*)

LARVA

PUPA

JIM SCHOLLMEYER

ADULT

JIM SCHOLLMEYER

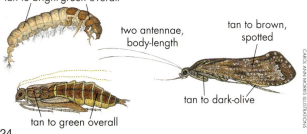

CADDISFLIES

In streams below dams or enriched by effluents or irrigation, the Spotted Sedge may *abound.* (And can be plentiful in any stream with lively currents.) Like the Gray Sedge (pages 22 and 23), the Spotted Sedge is important to the fly fisher in all three of its stages—the larva any time, the pupa during a hatch, and the adult when it returns to the water to lay its eggs.

tan to bright-green overall

two antennae, body-length

tan to brown, spotted

tan to dark-olive

tan to green overall

CAROL ANN MORRIS ILLUSTRATIONS

24

Important Stages: larva, pupa, adult

Seasonal Hatch Time: May through September

Daily Hatch Time: all day, sporadic. Egg-laying after-noon and evening

Hatch Conditions: any weather

Size: body 3/8 to 9/16 inch (10-14 mm). Hooks 16 to 10

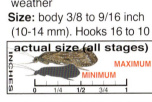

actual size (all stages)
INCHES
MAXIMUM
MINIMUM
0   1/4   1/2   3/4   1

Habitat: among rocks and debris in lively currents

Fishing Strategies: imitations of the larva may be good any time, but are especially promising early in the morning and in the evening when the real larvae may drift freely. Imitations of the pupa and adult are best during a hatch. Dry-fly imitations are best when the adults return to the water to lay their eggs

Spotted Sedge Typical Imitative Flies

Tan Caddis Larva   **Z-Wing Caddis Pupa**   **Kings River Caddis**

CADDISFLIES

| Caddisfly | OCTOBER CADDIS
(*Dicosmoecus*) |

LARVA

PUPA

ADULT

JIM SCHOLLMEYER

DAVE HUGHES

The October Caddis is the giant of common caddisflies of Western streams. Though its numbers are generally modest, it *can* hatch in abundance. Within its pebble-case the larva slowly transforms into a pupa; the pupa then abandons the case to swim to shore where it crawls out and hatches. Late in the day, egg-laying females skim and skitter across the water. Size makes this insect conspicuous, as does its appearance in fall when little else is hatching.

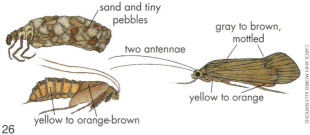

sand and tiny pebbles

two antennae

gray to brown, mottled

yellow to orange

yellow to orange-brown

CAROL ANN MORRIS ILLUSTRATIONS

Important Stages: larva, pupa, adult

Seasonal Hatch Time: September and October

Daily Hatch Time: all day. Females return late day

Hatch Conditions: all weather

Size: body 3/4 to 1 1/4 inch (20-30 mm). Hooks 10-6, long shank

Habitat: among stones in lively currents

Fishing Strategies: a larva-imitation fished dead drift can be effective any time. During the hatch, fish an imitation of the pupa either on a wet-fly swing or dead drift along the bottom. When adults are active in streamside brush and overhanging tree limbs, or when the egg-laying females return, fish a dry fly with nervous twitches

October Caddis Typical Imitative Flies

Deschutes Cased Caddis   **Dark Caddis Emergent**   **Orange Stimulator**

Midges

LARVA

PUPA

ADULT

"Midges," as they're commonly called on streams (on lakes they're called "chironomids"), are tiny and can hatch in good numbers, even in abundance, any time of the year. Midges look like mosquitos but lack the mosquito's bite. Size and form best identify midges since they can be almost any color (black, green, tan, brown, cream, red...). Midge hatches are most important in months when little else is hatching.

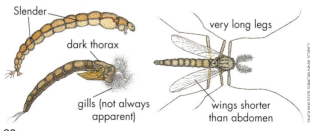

Slender

dark thorax

gills (not always apparent)

very long legs

wings shorter than abdomen

MIDGES

Important Stages: pupa, adult

Occasionally Important: larva

Seasonal Hatch Time: year round

Daily Hatch Time: all day, especially *late* day in warm months, midday in cold

Hatch Conditions: any weather

Size: body 1/16 to 1/4 inch (2-7 mm). Hooks 28-16

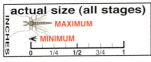

actual size (all stages)

INCHES

MAXIMUM

MINIMUM

0   1/4   1/2   3/4   1

Habitat: all currents and bottom types, but especially sunken debris

Fishing Strategies: though a difficult trout will sometimes fall for a deep imitation of the midge larva, most anglers fish a pupa-imitation barely submerged or an emerger-imitation or dry-fly adult dead drift to trout that are rising. Sometimes a *twitched* dry-fly is best

Midge Typical Imitative Flies

Palomino Midge   Griffith's Gnat   Cream Midge

MIDGES

SEASONAL HATCH CHART

To varying degrees, all insect hatches are undependable—they can be early or late by *weeks*. And bear in mind that stream hatches commonly come about a month earlier in the coastal states than in the states of the Rocky Mountains. The periods below show each hatch from its earliest start to its latest finish throughout the West.

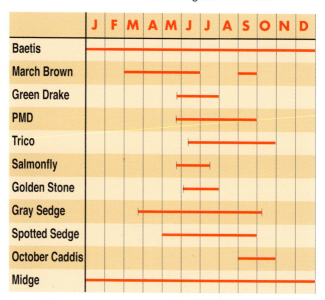

	J	F	M	A	M	J	J	A	S	O	N	D
Baetis	■	■	■	■	■	■	■	■	■	■	■	■
March Brown		■	■	■	■	■			■			
Green Drake					■	■	■					
PMD					■	■	■	■	■	■	■	■
Trico						■	■	■	■	■	■	■
Salmonfly					■	■						
Golden Stone					■	■	■					
Gray Sedge			■	■	■	■	■	■	■	■		
Spotted Sedge				■	■	■	■	■	■	■		
October Caddis									■	■	■	
Midge	■	■	■	■	■	■	■	■	■	■	■	■